How Do I Love Thee?

ELIZABETH BARRETT BROWNING

A Phoenix Paperback

Selected Poems by Elizabeth Barrett Browning
first published by J. M. Dent in 1988

This abridged edition published in 1996 by Phoenix,
a division of Orion Books Ltd,
Orion House, 5 Upper St Martin's Lane, London WC2H 9EA

Cover illustration: *April Love*, by Arthur Hughes,
Tate Gallery, London (Bridgeman Art Library, London)

ISBN 1 85799 655 0

Typeset by CentraCet Ltd, Cambridge
Printed in Great Britain by
Clays Ltd, St Ives plc

Contents

Catarina to Camoens

Dying in his absence abroad,
and referring to the poem in which
he recorded the sweetness of her eyes

I

On the door you will not enter,
　I have gazed too long – adieu!
Hope withdraws her peradventure –
　Death is near me, – and not *you*.
　　Come, O lover,
　　Close and cover
These poor eyes, you called, I ween,
'Sweetest eyes, were ever seen.'

II

When I heard you sing that burden
　In my vernal days and bowers,
Other praises disregarding,
　I but hearkened that of yours –
　　Only saying
　　In heart-playing,
'Blessed eyes mine eyes have been,
If the sweetest, HIS have seen!'

III

But all changes. At this vesper,
   'Cold the sun shines down the door.
If you stood there, would you whisper
   'Love, I love you,' as before, –
      Death pervading
      Now, and shading
Eyes you sang of, that yestreen,
As the sweetest ever seen?

IV

Yes, I think, were you beside them,
   Near the bed I die upon, –
Though their beauty you denied them,
   As you stood there, looking down,
      You would truly
      Call them duly,
For the love's sake found therein, –
'Sweetest eyes, were ever seen.'

V

And if *you* looked down upon them,
   And if *they* looked up to *you*,
All the light which has foregone them
   Would be gathered back anew.
      They would truly
      Be as duly

Love-transformed to beauty's sheen, –
'Sweetest eyes, were ever seen.'

VI

But, ah me! you only see me,
   In your thoughts of loving man,
Smiling soft perhaps and dreamy
   Through the wavings of my fan, –
     And unweeting
     Go repeating,
In your reverie serene,
'Sweetest eyes, were ever seen.'

VII

While my spirit leans and reaches
   From my body still and pale,
Fain to hear what tender speech is
   In your love to help my bale –
     O my poet,
     Come and show it!
Come, of latest love, to glean
'Sweetest eyes, were ever seen.'

VIII

O my poet, O my prophet,
   When you praised their sweetness so,
Did you think, in singing of it,
   That it might be near to go?

Had you fancies
From their glances,
That the grave would quickly screen
'Sweetest eyes, were ever seen'?

IX

No reply! the fountain's warble
  In the court-yard sounds alone.
As the water to the marble
  So my heart falls with a moan
    From love-sighing
    To this dying.
Death forerunneth Love to win
'Sweetest eyes, were ever seen.'

X

Will you come? When I'm departed
  Where all sweetnesses are hid;
Where thy voice, my tender-hearted,
  Will not lift up either lid.
    Cry, O lover,
    Love is over!
Cry beneath the cypress green –
'Sweetest eyes, were ever seen.'

XI

When the angelus is ringing,
  Near the convent will you walk,

And recall the choral singing
  Which brought angels down our talk?
    Spirit-shriven
    I viewed Heaven,
Till you smiled – 'Is earth unclean,
Sweetest eyes, were ever seen?'

XII

When beneath the palace-lattice,
  You ride slow as you have done,
And you see a face there – that is
  Not the old familiar one, –
    Will you oftly
    Murmur softly,
'Here, ye watched me morn and e'en,
Sweetest eyes, were ever seen'?

XIII

When the palace-ladies, sitting
  Round your gittern, shall have said,
'Poet, sing those verses written
  For the lady who is dead,'
    Will you tremble,
    Yet dissemble, –
Or sing hoarse, with tears between,
'Sweetest eyes, were ever seen'?

XIV

'Sweetest eyes!' how sweet in flowings
    The repeated cadence is!
Though you sang a hundred poems,
    Still the best one would be this.
        I can hear it
        'Twixt my spirit
And the earth-noise intervene –
'Sweetest eyes, were ever seen!'

XV

But the priest waits for the praying,
    And the choir are on their knees,
And the soul must pass away in
    Strains more solemn high than these.
        Miserere
        For the weary!
Oh, no longer for Catrine,
'Sweetest eyes, were ever seen!'

XVI

Keep my ribbon, take and keep it
    (I have loosed it from my hair),
Feeling, while you overweep it,
    Not alone in your despair,
        Since with saintly
        Watch unfaintly

Out of heaven shall o'er you lean
'Sweetest eyes, were ever seen.'

XVII

But – but *now* – yet unremovèd
   Up to Heaven, they glisten fast.
You may cast away, Belovèd,
   In your future all my past.
      Such old phrases
      May be praises
For some fairer bosom-queen –
'Sweetest eyes, were ever seen!'

XVIII

Eyes of mine, what are ye doing?
   Faithless, faithless, – praised amiss
If a tear be of your showing,
   Dropt for any hope of HIS!
      Death has boldness
      Besides coldness,
If unworthy tears demean
'Sweetest eyes, were ever seen.'

XIX

I will look out to his future;
   I will bless it till it shine.
Should he ever be a suitor
   Unto sweeter eyes than mine,

Sunshine gild them,
Angels shield them,
Whatsoever eyes terrene
Be the sweetest HIS have seen!

Hector in the Garden

I

Nine years old! The first of any
    Seem the happiest years that come:
Yet when *I* was nine, I said
    No such word! – I thought instead
That the Greeks had used as many
    In besieging Ilium.

II

Nine green years had scarcely brought me
    To my childhood's haunted spring:
I had life, like flowers and bees,
    In betwixt the country trees.
And the sun the pleasure taught me
    Which he teacheth every thing.

III

If the rain fell, there was sorrow,
    Little head leant on the pane,
8   Little finger drawing down it

The long trailing drops upon it,
  And the 'Rain, rain, come to-morrow,'
    Said for charm against the rain.

IV

Such a charm was right Canidian,
  Though you meet it with a jeer!
    If I said it long enough,
    Then the rain hummed dimly off,
And the thrush with his pure Lydian
  Was left only to the ear;

V

And the sun and I together
  Went a-rushing out of doors!
    We, our tender spirits, drew
    Over hill and dale in view,
Glimmering hither, glimmering thither,
  In the footsteps of the showers.

VI

Underneath the chestnuts dripping,
  Through the grasses wet and fair,
    Straight I sought my garden-ground
    With the laurel on the mound,
And the pear-tree oversweeping
  A side-shadow of green air.

VII

In the garden lay supinely
   A huge giant wrought of spade!
   Arms and legs were stretched at length
   In a passive giant strength, –
The fine meadow turf, cut finely,
   Round them laid and interlaid.

VIII

Call him Hector, son of Priam!
   Such his title and degree:
   With my rake I smoothed his brow,
   Both his cheeks I weeded through,
But a rimer such as I am
   Scarce can sing his dignity.

IX

Eyes of gentianellas azure,
   Staring, winking at the skies;
   Nose of gillyflowers and box;
   Scented grasses put for locks,
Which a little breeze, at pleasure,
   Set a-waving round his eyes.

X

Brazen helm of daffodillies,
   With a glitter toward the light;
   Purple violets for the mouth,

Breathing perfumes west and south;
And a sword of flashing lilies,
    Holden ready for the fight.

XI

And a breastplate made of daisies,
    Closely fitting, leaf on leaf;
    Periwinkles interlaced
    Drawn for belt about the waist;
While the brown bees, humming praises,
    Shot their arrows round the chief.

XII

And who knows (I sometimes wondered)
    If the disembodied soul
    Of old Hector, once of Troy,
    Might not take a dreary joy
Here to enter – if it thundered,
    Rolling up the thunder-roll?

XIII

Rolling this way from Troy-ruin,
    In this body rude and rife
    Just to enter, and take rest
    'Neath the daisies of the breast –
They, with tender roots, renewing
    His heroic heart to life?

XIV

Who could know? I sometimes started
    At a motion or a sound!
    Did his mouth speak – naming Troy,
    With an ὀτοτοτοτοῖ?
Did the pulse of the Strong-hearted
    Make the daisies tremble round?

XV

It was hard to answer, often:
    But the birds sang in the tree –
    But the little birds sang bold
    In the pear-tree green and old,
And my terror seemed to soften
    Through the courage of their glee.

XVI

Oh, the birds, the tree, the ruddy
    And white blossoms, sleek with rain!
    Oh, my garden, rich with pansies!
    Oh, my childhood's bright romances!
All revive, like Hector's body,
    And I see them stir again!

XVII

And despite life's changes – chances,
    And despite the deathbell's toll,
They press on me in full seeming!

Help, some angel! stay this dreaming!
  As the birds sang in the branches,
    Sing God's patience through my soul!

XVIII

That no dreamer, no neglecter
  Of the present's work unsped,
    I may wake up and be doing,
    Life's heroic ends pursuing,
Though my past is dead as Hector,
  And though Hector is twice dead.

A Woman's Shortcomings

I

She has laughed as softly as if she sighed,
  She has counted six, and over,
Of a purse well filled and a heart well tried –
  Oh, each a worthy lover!
They 'give her time;' for her soul must slip
  Where the world has set the grooving.
She will lie to none with her fair red lip, –
  But love seeks truer loving.

II

She trembles her fan in a sweetness dumb,
  As her thoughts were beyond recalling,

With a glance for *one*, and a glance for *some*,
   From her eyelids rising and falling;
Speaks common words with a blushful air,
   Hears bold words, unreproving;
But her silence says – what she never will swear –
   And love seeks better loving.

III

Go, lady, lean to the night-guitar
   And drop a smile to the bringer,
Then smile as sweetly, when he is far,
   At the voice of an in-door singer.
Bask tenderly beneath tender eyes;
   Glance lightly, on their removing;
And join new vows to old perjuries –
   But dare not call it loving.

IV

Unless you can think, when the song is done,
   No other is soft in the rhythm;
Unless you can feel, when left by One,
   That all men else go with him;
Unless you can know, when unpraised by his breath,
   That your beauty itself wants proving;
Unless you can swear 'For life, for death!' –
   Oh, fear to call it loving!

Unless you can muse in a crowd all day
  On the absent face that fixed you;
Unless you can love, as the angels may,
  With the breadth of heaven betwixt you;
Unless you can dream that his faith is fast,
  Through behoving and unbehoving;
Unless you can *die* when the dream is past –
  Oh, never call it loving!

from *Sonnets from the Portuguese*

I

I thought once how Theocritus had sung
Of the sweet years, the dear and wished-for years,
Who each one in a gracious hand appears
To bear a gift for mortals, old or young:
And, as I mused it in his antique tongue,
I saw, in gradual vision through my tears,
The sweet, sad years, the melancholy years,
Those of my own life, who by turns had flung
A shadow across me. Straightway I was 'ware,
So weeping, how a mystic Shape did move
Behind me, and drew me backward by the hair;
And a voice said in mastery, while I strove, –
'Guess now who holds thee?' – 'Death,' I said. But, there,
The silver answer rang, – 'Not Death, but Love.'

What can I give thee back, O liberal
And princely giver, who hast brought the gold
And purple of thine heart, unstained, untold,
And laid them on the outside of the wall
For such as I to take or leave withal,
In unexpected largesse? am I cold,
Ungrateful, that for these most manifold
High gifts, I render nothing back at all?
Not so; not cold, – but very poor instead.
Ask God who knows. For frequent tears have run
The colours from my life, and left so dead
And pale a stuff, it were not fitly done
To give the same as pillow to thy head.
Go farther! let it serve to trample on.

X

Yet, love, mere love, is beautiful indeed
And worthy of acceptation. Fire is bright,
Let temple burn, or flax. An equal light
Leaps in the flame from cedar-plank or weed.
And love is fire. And when I say at need
I love thee . . . mark! . . . *I love thee* – in thy sight
I stand transfigured, glorified aright,
With conscience of the new rays that proceed
Out of my face toward thine. There's nothing low
In love, when love the lowest: meanest creatures
Who love God, God accepts while loving so.

And what I *feel*, across the inferior features
Of what I *am*, doth flash itself, and show
How that great work of Love enhances Nature's.

XIV

If thou must love me, let it be for nought
Except for love's sake only. Do not say
'I love her for her smile . . . her look . . . her way
Of speaking gently, . . . for a trick of thought
That falls in well with mine, and certes brought
A sense of pleasant ease on such a day' –
For these things in themselves, Beloved, may
Be changed, or change for thee, – and love, so wrought
May be unwrought so. Neither love me for
Thine own dear pity's wiping my cheeks dry, –
A creature might forget to weep, who bore
Thy comfort long, and lose thy love thereby!
But love me for love's sake, that evermore
Thou may'st love on, through love's eternity.

XLIII

How do I love thee? Let me count the ways.
I love thee to the depth and breadth and height
My soul can reach, when feeling out of sight
For the ends of Being and ideal Grace.
I love thee to the level of everyday's
Most quiet need, by sun and candlelight.
I love thee freely, as men strive for Right;

I love thee purely, as they turn from Praise.
I love thee with the passion put to use
In my old griefs, and with my childhood's faith.
I love thee with a love I seemed to lose
With my lost saints, – I love thee with the breath,
Smiles, tears, of all my life! – and, if God choose,
I shall but love thee better after death.

from *Aurora Leigh*

Ten nights and days we voyaged on the deep;
Ten nights and days without the common face
Of any day or night; the moon and sun
Cut off from the green reconciling earth,
To starve into a blind ferocity
And glare unnatural; the very sky
·   (Dropping its bell-net down upon the sea,
As if no human heart should 'scape alive)
Bedraggled with the desolating salt,
Until it seemed no more that holy heaven
To which my father went. All new and strange;
The universe turned stranger, for a child.

Then, land! – then, England! oh, the frosty cliffs
Looked cold upon me. Could I find a home
Among those mean red houses through the fog?
And when I heard my father's language first

From alien lips which had no kiss for mine
I wept aloud, then laughed, then wept, then wept,
And someone near me said the child was mad
Through much sea-sickness. The train swept us on:
Was this my father's England? the great isle?
The ground seemed cut up from the fellowship
Of verdure, field from field, as man from man;
The skies themselves looked low and positive,
As almost you could touch them with a hand,
And dared to do it they were so far off
From God's celestial crystals; all things blurred
And dull and vague. Did Shakespeare and his mates
Absorb the light here? – not a hill or stone
With heart to strike a radiant colour up
Or active outline on the indifferent air.

I think I see my father's sister stand
Upon the hall-step of her country-house
To give me welcome. She stood straight and calm,
Her somewhat narrow forehead braided tight
As if for taming accidental thoughts
From possible pulses; brown hair pricked with gray
By frigid use of life (she was not old,
Although my father's elder by a year),
A nose drawn sharply, yet in delicate lines;
A close mild mouth, a little soured about
The ends, through speaking unrequited loves
Or peradventure niggardly half-truths;

Eyes of no colour, – once they might have smiled,
But never, never have forgot themselves
In smiling; cheeks, in which was yet a rose
Of perished summers, like a rose in a book,
Kept more for ruth than pleasure, – if past bloom,
Past fading also.

                She had lived, we'll say,
A harmless life, she called a virtuous life,
A quiet life, which was not life at all
(But that, she had not lived enough to know),
Between the vicar and the county squires,
The lord-lieutenant looking down sometimes
From the empyrean to assure their souls
Against chance vulgarisms, and, in the abyss,
The apothecary, looked on once a year
To prove their soundness of humility.
The poor-club exercised her Christian gifts
Of knitting stockings, stitching petticoats,
Because we are of one flesh, afterall,
And need one flannel (with a proper sense
Of difference in the quality) – and still
The book-club, guarded from your modern trick
Of shaking dangerous questions from the crease,
Preserved her intellectual. She had lived
A sort of cage-bird life, born in a cage,
Accounting that to leap from perch to perch
Was act and joy enough for any bird.
Dear heaven, how silly are the things that live

In thickets, and eat berries!
                    I alas,
A wild bird scarcely fledged, was brought to her
        cage,
And she was there to meet me. Very kind.
Bring the clean water, give out the fresh seed.

She stood upon the steps to welcome me,
Calm, in black garb. I clung about her neck, –
Young babes, who catch at every shred of wool
To draw the new light closer, catch and cling
Less blindly. In my ears my father's word
Hummed ignorantly, as the sea in shells,
'Love, love, my child.' She, black there with my grief,
Might feel my love – she was his sister once –
I clung to her. A moment she seemed moved,
Kissed me with cold lips, suffered me to cling,
And drew me feebly through the hall into
The room she sat in.
                    There, with some strange spasm
Of pain and passion, she wrung loose my hands
Imperiously, and held me at arm's length,
And with two grey-steel naked-bladed eyes
Searched through my face, – ay, stabbed it through and
        through,
Through brows and cheeks and chin, as if to find
A wicked murderer in my innocent face,
If not here, there perhaps. Then, drawing breath,

She struggled for her ordinary calm –
And missed it rather, – told me not to shrink,
As if she had told me not to lie or swear, –
'She loved my father and would love me too
As long as I deserved it.' Very kind.

I understood her meaning afterward;
She thought to find my mother in my face,
And questioned it for that. For she, my aunt,
Had loved my father truly, as she could,
And hated, with the gall of gentle souls,
My Tuscan mother who had fooled away
A wise man from wise courses, a good man
From obvious duties, and, depriving her,
His sister, of the household precedence,
Had wronged his tenants, robbed his native land,
And made him mad, alike by life and death,
In love and sorrow. She had pored for years
What sort of woman could be suitable
To her sort of hate, to entertain it with,
And so, her very curiosity
Became hate too, and all the idealism
She ever used in life was used for hate,
Till hate, so nourished, did exceed at last
The love from which it grew, in strength and heat,
And wrinkled her smooth conscience with a sense
Of disputable virtue (say not, sin)
When Christian doctrine was enforced at church.

And thus my father's sister was to me
My mother's hater. From that day she did
Her duty to me (I appreciate it
In her own word as spoken to herself),
Her duty, in large measure, well pressed out,
But measured always. She was generous, bland,
More courteous than was tender, gave me still
The first place, – as if fearful that God's saints
Would look down suddenly and say, 'Herein
You missed a point, I think, through lack of love.'
Alas, a mother never is afraid
Of speaking angerly to any child,
Since love, she knows, is justified of love.
And I, I was a good child on the whole,
A meek and manageable child. Why not?
I did not live, to have the faults of life:
There seemed more true life in my father's grave
Than in all England. Since *that* threw me off
Who fain would cleave (his latest will, they say,
Consigned me to his land), I only thought
Of lying quiet there where I was thrown
Like sea-weed on the rocks, and suffering her
To prick me to a pattern with her pin,
Fibre from fibre, delicate leaf from leaf,
And dry out from my drowned anatomy
The last sea-salt left in me.
                              So it was.
I broke the copious curls upon my head

In braids, because she liked smooth-ordered hair.
I left off saying my sweet Tuscan words
Which still at any stirring of the heart
Came up to float across the English phrase
As lilies (*Bene* or *Che che*), because
She liked my father's child to speak his tongue.
I learnt the collects and the catechism,
The creeds, from Athanasius back to Nice,
The Articles, the Tracts *against* the times
(By no means Buonaventure's 'Prick of Love'),
And various popular synopses of
Inhuman doctrines never taught by John,
Because she liked instructed piety.
I learnt my complement of classic French
(Kept pure of Balzac and neologism)
And German also, since she liked a range
Of liberal education, – tongues, not books.
I learnt a little algebra, a little
Of the mathematics, – brushed with extreme flounce
The circle of sciences, because
She misliked women who are frivolous.
I learnt the royal genealogies
Of Oviedo, the internal laws
Of the Burmese empire, – by how many feet
Mount Chimborazo outsoars Teneriffe,
What navigable river joins itself
To Lara, and what census of the year five

Was taken at Klagenfurt, – because she liked

A general insight into useful facts,
I learnt much music, – such as would have been
As quite impossible in Johnson's day
As still it might be wished – fine sleights of hand
And unimagined fingering, shuffling off
The hearer's soul through hurricanes of notes
To a noisy Tophet; and I drew . . . costumes
From French engravings, nereids neatly draped
(With smirks of simmering godship): I washed in
Landscapes from nature (rather say, washed out).
I danced the polka and Cellarius,
Spun glass, stuffed birds, and modelled flowers in
     wax,
Because she liked accomplishments in girls.
I read a score of books on womanhood
To prove, if women do not think at all,
They may teach thinking (to a maiden aunt
Or else the author), – books that boldly assert
Their right of comprehending husband's talk
When not too deep, and even of answering
With pretty 'may it please you', or 'so it is', –
Their rapid insight and fine aptitude,
Particular worth and general missionariness,
As long as they keep quiet by the fire
And never say 'no' when the world says 'ay',
For that is fatal, – their angelic reach
Of virtue, chiefly used to sit and darn,
And fatten household sinners, – their, in brief,

Potential faculty in everything
Of abdicating power in it: she owned
She liked a woman to be womanly,
And, English women, she thanked God and sighed
(Some people always sigh in thanking God),
Were models to the universe. And last
I learnt cross-stitch, because she did not like
To see me wear the night with empty hands
A-doing nothing. So, my shepherdess
Was something after all (the pastoral saints
Be praised for't), leaning lovelorn with pink eyes
To match her shoes, when I mistook the silks;
Her head uncrushed by that round weight of hat
So strangely similar to the tortoise-shell
Which slew the tragic poet.

                    By the way,
The works of women are symbolical.
We sew, sew, prick our fingers, dull our sight,
Producing what? A pair of slippers, sir,
To put on when you're weary – or a stool
To stumble over and vex you . . . 'curse that stool!'
Or else at best, a cushion, where you lean
And sleep, and dream of something we are not
But would be for your sake. Alas, alas!
This hurts most, this – that after all we are paid
The worth of our work, perhaps.

                    In looking down
Those years of education (to return)

I wondered if Brinvilliers suffered more
In the water-torture . . . flood succeeding flood
To drench the incapable throat and split the veins . . .
Than I did. Certain of your feebler souls
Go out in such a process; many pine
To a sick inodorous light; my own endured:
I had relations in the Unseen, and drew
The elemental nutriment and heat
From nature, as earth feels the sun at nights,
Or as a babe sucks surely in the dark.
I kept the life thrust on me, on the outside
Of the inner life with all its ample room
For heart and lungs, for will and intellect,
Inviolable by conventions . . .

My books! At last because the time was ripe,
I chanced upon the poets.

                    As the earth
Plunges in fury, when the internal fires
Have reached and pricked her heart, and throwing
    flat
The marts and temples, the triumphal gates
And towers of observation, clears herself
To elemental freedom – thus, my soul,
At poetry's divine first finger-touch,
Let go conventions and sprang up surprised,
Convicted of the great eternities
Before two worlds.

What's this, Aurora Leigh,
You write so of the poets, and not laugh?
Those virtuous liars, dreamers after dark,
Exaggerators of the sun and moon,
And soothsayers in a tea-cup?

                      I write so
Of the only truth-tellers now left to God,
The only speakers of essential truth,
Opposed to relative, comparative,
And temporal truths; the only holders by
His sun-skirts, through conventional gray glooms;
The only teachers who instruct mankind
From just a shadow on a charnel-wall
To find man's veritable stature out
Erect, sublime, – the measure of a man,
And that's the measure of an angel, says
The apostle. Ay, and while your common men
Lay telegraphs, gauge railroads, reign, reap, dine,
And dust the flaunty carpets of the world
For kings to walk on, or our president,
The poet suddenly will catch them up
With his voice like a thunder, – 'This is soul,
This is life, this word is being said in heaven,
Here's God down on us! What are you about?'
How all those workers start amid their work,
Look round, look up, and feel a moment's space,
That carpet-dusting, though a pretty trade,
Is not the imperative labour after all.

My own best poets, am I one with you,
That thus I love you, – or but one through love?
Does all this smell of thyme about my feet
Conclude my visit to your holy hill
In personal presence, or but testify
The rustling of your vesture through my dreams
With influent odours? Why my joy and pain,
My thought and aspiration, like the stops
Of pipe or flute, are absolutely dumb
Unless melodious, do you play on me
My pipers, – and if, sooth, you did not blow,
Would no sound come? or is the music mine,
As a man's voice or breath is called his own,
Inbreathed by the Life-breather? There's a doubt
For cloudy seasons!

              But the sun was high
When first I felt my pulses set themselves
For concord; when the rhythmic turbulence
Of blood and brain swept outward upon words,
As wind upon the alders, blanching them
By turning up their under-natures till
They trembled in dilation. O delight
And triumph of the poet, who would say
A man's mere 'yes', a woman's common 'no',
A little human hope of that or this,
And says the word so that it burns you through
With a special revelation, shakes the heart
Of all the men and women in the world,

As if one came back from the dead and spoke,
With eyes too happy, a familiar thing
Become divine i' the utterance! while for him
The poet, speaker, he expands with joy;
The palpitating angel in his flesh
Thrills inly with consenting fellowship
To those innumerous spirits who sun themselves
Outside of time.
                    O life, O poetry,
– Which means life in life! cognisant of life
Beyond this blood-beat, passionate for truth
Beyond these senses! – poetry, my life,
My eagle, with both grappling feet still hot
From Zeus' thunder, who hast ravished me
Away from all the shepherds, sheep, and dogs,
And set me in the Olympian roar and round
Of luminous faces for a cup-bearer,
To keep the mouths of all the godheads moist
For everlasting laughters, – I myself
Half drunk across the beaker with their eyes!
How those gods look!
                        Enough so, Ganymede,
We shall not bear above a round or two.
We drop the golden cup at Hebe's foot
And swoon back to the earth, – and find ourselves
Face-down among the pine-cones, cold with dew,
While the dogs bark, and many a shepherd scoffs,
'What's come now to the youth?' Ups and downs

Have poets.
                    Am I such indeed? The name
Is royal, and to sign it like a queen
Is what I dare not, – though some royal blood
Would seem to tingle in me now and then,
With sense of power and ache, – with imposthumes
And manias usual to the race. Howbeit
I dare not; 'tis too easy to go mad
And ape a Bourbon in a crown of straws;
The thing's too common.
                              Many fervent souls
Strike rhyme on rhyme, who would strike steel on steel
If steel had offered, in a restless heat
Of doing something. Many tender souls
Have strung their losses on a rhyming thread,
As children cowslips; – the more pains they take,
The work more withers. Young men, ay, and maids,
Too often sow their wild oats in tame verse,
Before they sit down under their own vine
And live for use. Alas, near all the birds
Will sing at dawn, – and yet we do not take
The chaffering swallow for the holy lark.
In those days, though, I never analysed,
Not even myself. Analysis comes late.
You catch a sight of Nature, earliest,
In full front sun-face, and your eyelids wink
And drop before the wonder of't; you miss
The form, through seeing the light. I lived, those days,

And wrote because I lived – unlicensed else;
My heart beat in my brain. Life's violent flood
Abolished bounds, – and, which my neighbour's field,
Which mine, what mattered? It is thus in youth!
We play at leap-frog over the god Term;
The love within us and the love without
Are mixed, confounded; if we are loved or love
We scarce distinguish: thus, with other power;
Being acted on and acting seem the same:
In that first onrush of life's chariot-wheels,
We know not if the forests move or we.

And so, like most young poets, in a flush
Of individual life I poured myself
Along the veins of others, and achieved
Mere lifeless imitations of live verse,
And made the living answer for the dead,
Profaning nature. 'Touch not, do not taste,
Nor handle,' – we're too legal, who write young:
We beat the phorminx till we hurt our thumbs,
As if still ignorant of counterpoint;
We call the Muse, – 'O Muse, benignant Muse,' –
As if we had seen her purple-braided head,
With the eyes in it, start between the boughs
As often as a stag's. What make-believe,
With so much earnest! what effete results
From virile efforts! what cold wire-drawn odes
From such white heats! – bucolics, where the cows

Would scare the writer if they splashed the mud
In lashing off the flies, – didactics, driven
Against the heels of what the master said;
And counterfeiting epics, shrill with trumps
A babe might blow between two straining cheeks
Of bubbled rose, to make his mother laugh;
And elegiac griefs, and songs of love,
Like cast-off nosegays picked up on the road,
The worse for being warm: all these things, writ
On happy mornings, with a morning heart,
That leaps for love, is active for resolve,
Weak for art only. Oft, the ancient forms
Will thrill, indeed, in carrying the young blood,
The wine-skins, now and then, a little warped,
Will crack even, as the new wine gurgles in.
Spare the old bottles! – spill not the new wine.

By Keats's soul, the man who never stepped
In gradual progress like another man,
But, turning grandly on his central self,
Ensphered himself in twenty perfect years
And died, not young (the life of a long life
Distilled to a mere drop, falling like a tear
Upon the world's cold cheek to make it burn
For ever); by that strong excepted soul,
I count it strange and hard to understand
That nearly all young poets should write old,
That Pope was sexagenary at sixteen,

And beardless Byron academical,
And so with others. It may be perhaps
Such have not settled long and deep enough
In trance, to attain to clairvoyance, – and still
The memory mixes with the vision, spoils,
And works it turbid.

                Or perhaps, again,
In order to discover the Muse-Sphinx,
The melancholy desert must sweep round,
Behind you as before. –

                      For me, I wrote
False poems, like the rest, and thought them true
Because myself was true in writing them.
I peradventure have writ true ones since
With less complacence.

                   But I could not hide
My quickening inner life from those at watch.
They saw a light at a window, now and then,
They had not set there: who had set it there?
My father's sister started when she caught
My soul agaze in my eyes. She could not say
I had no business with a sort of soul,
But plainly she objected, – and demurred
That souls were dangerous things to carry straight
Through all the spilt saltpetre of the world.
She said sometimes, 'Aurora, have you done
Your task this morning? have you read that book?
And are you ready for the crochet here?' –

As if she said, 'I know there's something wrong;
I know I have not ground you down enough
To flatten and bake you to a wholesome crust
For household uses and proprieties,
Before the rain has got into my barn
And set the grains a-sprouting. What, you're green
With out-door impudence? You almost grow?'
To which I answered, 'Would she hear my task,
And verify my abstract of the book?
Or should I sit down to the crochet work?
Was such her pleasure?' Then I sat and teased
The patient needle till it split the thread,
Which oozed off from it in meandering lace
From hour to hour. I was not, therefore, sad;
My soul was singing at a work apart
Behind the wall of sense, as safe from harm
As sings the lark when sucked up out of sight
In vortices of glory and blue air.

And so, through forced work and spontaneous work,
The inner life informed the outer life,
Reduced the irregular blood to a settled rhythm,
Made cool the forehead with fresh-sprinkling
        dreams,
And, rounding to the spheric soul the thin,
Pined body, struck a colour up the cheeks
Though somewhat faint . . .

from *Casa Guidi Windows*

You enter, in your Florence wanderings,
    The church of St. Maria Novella. Pass
The left stair, where at plague-time Macchiavel
    Saw One with set fair face as in a glass,
Dressed out against the fear of death and hell,
    Rustling her silks in pauses of the mass,
To keep the thought off how her husband fell,
    When she left home, stark dead across her feet, –
The stair leads up to what the Orgagnas save
    Of Dante's dæmons; you, in passing it,
Ascend the right stair from the farther nave,
    To muse in a small chapel scarcely lit
By Cimabue's Virgin. Bright and brave,
    That picture was accounted, mark, of old.
A king stood bare before its sovran grace,
    A reverent people shouted to behold
The picture, not the king, and even the place
    Containing such a miracle, grew bold,
Named the Glad Borgo from that beauteous face, –
    Which thrilled the artist, after work, to think
His own ideal Mary-smile should stand
    So very near him, – he, within the brink
Of all that glory, let in by his hand
    With too divine a rashness! Yet none shrink
36   Who come to gaze here now – albeit 'twas planned

Sublimely in the thought's simplicity.
The Lady, throned in empyreal state,
   Minds only the young babe upon her knee,
While sidelong angels bear the royal weight,
   Prostrated meekly, smiling tenderly
Oblivion of their wings; the Child thereat
   Stretching its hand like God. If any should,
Because of some stiff draperies and loose joints,
   Gaze scorn down from the heights of Raffaelhood,
On Cimabue's picture, – Heaven anoints
   The head of no such critic, and his blood
The poet's curse strikes full on and appoints
   To ague and cold spasms for evermore.
A noble picture! worthy of the shout
   Wherewith along the streets the people bore
Its cherub faces, which the sun threw out
   Until they stooped and entered the church door! –
Yet rightly was young Giotto talked about,
   Whom Cimabue found among the sheep,
And knew, as gods know gods, and carried home
   To paint the things he had painted, with a deep
And fuller insight, and so overcome
   His chapel-lady with a heavenlier sweep
Of light. For thus we mount into the sum
   Of great things known or acted. I hold, too,
That Cimabue smiled upon the lad,
   At the first stroke which passed what he could do, –
Or else his Virgin's smile had never had

Such sweetness in 't. All great men who foreknew
Their heirs in art, for art's sake have been glad,
    And bent their old white heads as if uncrowned,
Fanatics of their pure ideals still
    Far more than of their triumphs, which were found
With some less vehement struggle of the will.
    If old Margheritone trembled, swooned,
And died despairing at the open sill
    Of other men's achievements, (who achieved,
By loving art beyond the master!) he
    Was old Margheritone, and conceived
Never, at first youth and most ecstasy,
    A Virgin like that dream of one, which heaved
The death-sigh from his heart. If wistfully
    Margheritone sickened at the smell
Of Cimabue's laurel, let him go! –
    For Cimabue stood up very well
In spite of Giotto's – and Angelico,
    The artist-saint, kept smiling in his cell
The smile with which he welcomed the sweet slow
    Inbreak of angels, (whitening through the dim
That he might paint them!) while the sudden sense
    Of Raffael's future was revealed to him
By force of his own fair works' competence.
    The same blue waters where the dolphins swim
Suggest the tritons. Through the blue Immense,
    Strike out, all swimmers! cling not in the way
Of one another, so to sink; but learn

The strong man's impulse, catch the fresh'ning spray
He throws up in his motions, and discern
  By his clear, westering eye, the time of day.
Thou, God, hast set us worthy gifts to earn,
  Besides thy heaven and Thee! and when I say
There's room here for the weakest man alive
  To live and die, – there's room too, I repeat,
For all the strongest to live well, and strive
  Their own way, by their individual heat, –
Like some new bee-swarm leaving the old hive,
  Despite the wax which tempts so violet-sweet.
Then let the living live, the dead retain
  Their grave-cold flowers! – though honour's best
    supplied,
By bringing actions, to prove theirs not vain.

  Cold graves, we say? It shall be testified
That living men who burn in heart and brain,
  Without the dead were colder. If we tried
To sink the past beneath our feet, be sure
  The future would not stand. Precipitate
This old roof from the shrine – and, insecure,
  The nesting swallows fly off, mate from mate.
How scant the gardens, if the graves were fewer!
  The tall green poplars grew no longer straight,
Whose tops not looked to Troy. Would any fight
  For Athens, and not swear by Marathons
Who dared build temples, without tombs in sight?

Or live, without some dead man's benison?
Or seek truth, hope for good, and strive for right,
    If, looking up, he saw not in the sun
Some angel of the martyrs all day long
    Standing and waiting? Your last rhythm will need
Your earliest key-note. Could I sing this song,
    If my dead masters had not taken heed
To help the heavens and earth to make me strong,
    As the wind ever will find out some reed,
And touch it to such issues as belong
    To such a frail thing? None may grudge the dead,
Libations from full cups. Unless we choose
    To look back to the hills behind us spread,
The plains before us, sadden and confuse;
    If orphaned, we are disinherited.

I would but turn these lachrymals to use,
    And pour fresh oil in from the olive grove,
To furnish them as new lamps. Shall I say
    What made my heart beat with exulting love,
A few weeks back? –
                            . . . . The day was such a day
    As Florence owes the sun. The sky above,
Its weight upon the mountains seemed to lay,
    And palpitate in glory, like a dove
Who has flown too fast, full-hearted! – take away
    The image! for the heart of man beat higher
That day in Florence, flooding all her streets

And piazzas with a tumult and desire.
The people, with accumulated heats,
    And faces turned one way, as if one fire
Both drew and flushed them, left their ancient beats,
    And went up toward the palace-Pitti wall,
To thank their Grand-duke, who, not quite of course,
    Had graciously permitted, at their call,
The citizens to use their civic force
    To guard their civic homes. So, one and all,
The Tuscan cities streamed up to the source
    Of this new good, at Florence, taking it
As good so far, presageful of more good, –
    The first torch of Italian freedom, lit
To toss in the next tiger's face who should
    Approach too near them in a greedy fit, –
The first pulse of an even flow of blood,
    To prove the level of Italian veins
Toward rights perceived and granted. How we gazed
    From Casa Guidi windows, while, in trains
Of orderly procession – banners raised,
    And intermittent burst of martial strains
Which died upon the shout, as if amazed
    By gladness beyond music – they passed on!
The Magistracy, with insignia, passed, –
    And all the people shouted in the sun,
And all the thousand windows which had cast
    A ripple of silks, in blue and scarlet, down,
(As if the houses overflowed at last,)

Seemed growing larger with fair heads and eyes.
The Lawyers passed, – and still arose the shout,
And hands broke from the windows to surprise
Those grave calm brows with bay-tree leaves thrown
out.
The Priesthood passed, – the friars with worldly-wise
Keen sidelong glances from their beards about
The street to see who shouted! many a monk
Who takes a long rope in the waist, was there!
Whereat the popular exultation drunk
With indrawn divas' the whole sunny air,
While, through the murmuring windows, rose and
sunk
A cloud of kerchiefed hands, – 'The church makes fair
Her welcome in the new Pope's name.' Ensued
The black sign of the 'Martyrs!' (name no name,
But count the graves in silence.) Next, were viewed
The Artists; next, the Trades; and after came
The People, – flag and sign, and rights as good, –
And very loud the shout was for that same
Motto, 'Il popolo.' Il Popolo, –
The word means dukedom, empire, majesty,
And kings in such an hour might read it so.
And next, with banners, each in his degree,
Deputed representatives a-row
Of every separate state of Tuscany.
Siena's she-wolf, bristling on the fold

Of the first flag, preceded Pisa's hare,

And Massa's lion floated calm in gold,
Pienza's following with his silver stare.
    Arezzo's steed pranced clear from bridle-hold, –
And well might shout our Florence, greeting there
    These, and more brethren. Last, the world had sent
The various children of her teeming flanks –
    Greeks, English, French – as if to a parliament
Of lovers of her Italy in ranks,
    Each bearing its land's symbol reverent.
At which the stones seemed breaking into thanks
    And rattling up the sky, such sounds in proof
Arose; the very house-walls seemed to bend;
    The very windows, up from door to roof,
Flashed out a rapture of bright heads, to mend
    With passionate looks, the gesture's whirling off
A hurricane of leaves. Three hours did end
    While all these passed; and ever in the crowd,
Rude men, unconscious of the tears that kept
    Their beards moist, shouted; some few laughed aloud,
And none asked any why they laughed and wept.
    Friends kissed each other's cheeks, and foes long
        vowed
More warmly did it, – two-months' babies leapt
    Right upward in their mother's arms, whose black,
Wide, glittering eyes looked elsewhere; lovers pressed
    Each before either, neither glancing back;
And peasant maidens, smoothly 'tired and tressed,
    Forgot to finger on their throats the slack

Great pearl-strings; while old blind men would not rest,
    But pattered with their staves and slid their shoes
Along the stones, and smiled as if they saw.
    O heaven, I think that day had noble use
Among God's days. So near stood Right and Law,
    Both mutually forborne! Law would not bruise,
Nor Right deny, and each in reverent awe
    Honoured the other. And if, ne'ertheless,
That good day's sun delivered to the vines
    No charta, and the liberal Duke's excess
Did scarce exceed a Guelf's or Ghibelline's
    In any special actual righteousness
Of what that day he granted, still the signs
    Are good and full of promise, we must say,
When multitudes approach their kings with prayers
    And kings concede their people's right to pray,
Both in one sunshine. Griefs are not despairs,
    So uttered, nor can royal claims dismay
When men from humble homes and ducal chairs,
    Hate wrong together. It was well to view
Those banners ruffled in a ruler's face
    Inscribed, 'Live freedom, union, and all true
Brave patriots who are aided by God's grace!'
    Nor was it ill, when Leopoldo drew
His little children to the window-place
    He stood in at the Pitti, to suggest
They too should govern as the people willed.
    What a cry rose then! some, who saw the best,

Declared his eyes filled up and overfilled
    With good warm human tears which unrepressed
Ran down. I like his face; the forehead's build
    Has no capacious genius, yet perhaps
Sufficient comprehension, – mild and sad,
    And careful nobly, – not with care that wraps
Self-loving hearts, to stifle and make mad,
    But careful with the care that shuns a lapse
Of faith and duty, studious not to add
    A burden in the gathering of a gain.
And so, God save the Duke, I say with those
    Who that day shouted it, and while dukes reign,
May all wear in the visible overflows
    Of spirit, such a look of careful pain!
For God must love it better than repose.

And all the people who went up to let
    Their hearts out to that Duke, as has been told –
Where guess ye that the living people met,
    Kept tryst, formed ranks, chose leaders, first unrolled
Their banners?
                                In the Loggia? where is set
    Cellini's godlike Perseus, bronze – or gold –
(How name the metal, when the statue flings
    Its soul so in your eyes?) with brow and sword
Superbly calm, as all opposing things,
    Slain with the Gorgon, were no more abhorred
Since ended?

　　　　　　No, the people sought no wings
　　From Perseus in the Loggia, nor implored
An inspiration in the place beside,
　　From that dim bust of Brutus, jagged and
　　　　grand,
Where Buonarroti passionately tried
　　From out the close-clenched marble to demand
The head of Rome's sublimest homicide, –
　　Then dropt the quivering mallet from his hand,
Despairing he could find no model-stuff

The Cry of the Children

I

Do ye hear the children weeping, O my brothers,
　　　　Ere the sorrow comes with years?
They are leaning their young heads against their
　　　　mothers,
　　　　　　And *that* cannot stop their tears.
The young lambs are bleating in the meadows,
　　The young birds are chirping in the nest,
The young fawns are playing with the shadows,
　　The young flowers are blowing toward the west –
But the young, young children, O my brothers,
　　　　　　They are weeping bitterly!
They are weeping in the playtime of the others,
　　　　　　In the country of the free.

II

Do you question the young children in the sorrow
    Why their tears are falling so?
The old man may weep for his to-morrow
    Which is lost in Long Ago;
The old tree is leafless in the forest,
  The old year is ending in the frost,
The old wound, if stricken, is the sorest,
  The old hope is hardest to be lost.
But the young, young children, O my brothers,
    Do you ask them why they stand
Weeping sore before the bosoms of their mothers,
    In our happy Fatherland?

III

They look up with their pale and sunken faces,
    And their looks are sad to see,
For the man's hoary anguish draws and presses
    Down the cheeks of infancy.
'Your old earth,' they say, 'is very dreary;
  Our young feet,' they say, 'are very weak!
Few paces have we taken, yet are weary –
  Our grave-rest is very far to seek.
Ask the aged why they weep, and not the children;
    For the outside earth is cold;
And we young ones stand without, in our bewildering,
    And the graves are for the old.'

IV

'True,' say the children, 'it may happen
    That we die before our time;
Little Alice died last year – her grave is shapen
    Like a snowball, in the rime.
We looked into the pit prepared to take her:
    Was no room for any work in the close clay!
From the sleep wherein she lieth none will wake her,
    Crying, "Get up, little Alice! it is day."
If you listen by that grave, in sun and shower,
    With your ear down, little Alice never cries;
Could we see her face, be sure we should not know her,
    For the smile has time for growing in her eyes:
And merry go her moments, lulled and stilled in
    The shroud by the kirk-chime.
'It is good when it happens,' say the children,
    'That we die before our time.'

V

Alas, alas, the children! they are seeking
    Death in life, as best to have;
They are binding up their hearts away from breaking,
    With a cerement from the grave.
Go out, children, from the mine and from the city,
    Sing out, children, as the little thrushes do;
Pluck you handfuls of the meadow-cowslips pretty,
    Laugh aloud, to feel your fingers let them through !
But they answer, 'Are your cowslips of the meadows

Like our weeds anear the mine?
Leave us quiet in the dark of the coal-shadows,
    From your pleasures fair and fine!

VI

'For oh,' say the children, 'we are weary,
    And we cannot run or leap;
If we cared for any meadows, it were merely
    To drop down in them and sleep.
Our knees tremble sorely in the stooping,
    We fall upon our faces, trying to go;
And, underneath our heavy eyelids drooping,
    The reddest flower would look as pale as snow;
For, all day, we drag our burden tiring
    Through the coal-dark, underground –
Or, all day, we drive the wheels of iron
    In the factories, round and round.

VII

'For all day, the wheels are droning, turning;
    Their wind comes in our faces, –
Till our hearts turn, – our heads with pulses burning,
    And the walls turn in their places:
Turns the sky in the high window blank and reeling,
    Turns the long light that drops adown the wall,
Turn the black flies that crawl along the ceiling,
    All are turning, all the day, and we with all.
And all day, the iron wheels are droning,

And sometimes we could pray,
"O ye wheels," (breaking out in a mad moaning)
    "Stop! be silent for to-day!" '

VIII

Aye, be silent! Let them hear each other breathing
    For a moment, mouth to mouth!
Let them touch each other's hands, in a fresh wreathing
    Of their tender human youth!
Let them feel that this cold metallic motion
    Is not all the life God fashions or reveals:
Let them prove their living souls against the notion
    That they live in you, or under you, O wheels! –
Still, all day, the iron wheels go onward,
    Grinding life down from its mark;
And the children's souls, which God is calling sunward,
    Spin on blindly in the dark.

IX

Now tell the poor young children, O my brothers,
    To look up to Him and pray;
So the blessed One who blesseth all the others,
    Will bless them another day.
They answer, 'Who is God that He should hear us,
    While the rushing of the iron wheels is stirred?
When we sob aloud, the human creatures near us
    Pass by, hearing not, or answer not a word.
50   And *we* hear not (for the wheels in their resounding)

Strangers speaking at the door:
Is it likely God, with angels singing round him,
    Hears our weeping any more?

X

'Two words, indeed, of praying we remember,
    And at midnight's hour of harm,
"Our Father," looking upward in the chamber,
    We say softly for a charm.
We know no other words except "Our Father,"
    And we think that, in some pause of angels' song,
God may pluck them with the silence sweet to gather,
    And hold both within His right hand which is strong.
"Our Father!" If He heard us, He would surely
    (For they call Him good and mild)
Answer, smiling down the steep world very purely,
    "Come and rest with Me, My child."'

XI

'But no!' say the children, weeping faster,
    'He is speechless as a stone:
And they tell us, of His image is the master
    Who commands us to work on.
Go to!' say the children, – 'up in heaven,
    Dark, wheel-like, turning clouds are all we find.
Do not mock us; grief has made us unbelieving –
    We look up for God, but tears have made us blind.'
Do you hear the children weeping and disproving,

O my brothers, what ye preach?
For God's possible is taught by His world's loving,
And the children doubt of each.

XII

And well may the children weep before you!
    They are weary ere they run;
They have never seen the sunshine, nor the glory
    Which is brighter than the sun.
They know the grief of man, without its wisdom;
    They sink in man's despair, without its calm;
Are slaves, without the liberty in Christdom,
    Are martyrs, by the pang without the palm, –
Are worn as if with age, yet unretrievingly
    The harvest of its memories cannot reap, –
Are orphans of the earthly love and heavenly.
    Let them weep! let them weep!

XIII

They look up with their pale and sunken faces,
    And their look is dread to see,
For they mind you of their angels in high places,
    With eyes turned on Deity! –
'How long,' they say, 'how long, O cruel nation,
    Will you stand, to move the world, on a child's
        heart, –
Stifle down with a mailed heel its palpitation,
    And tread onward to your throne amid the mart?

Our blood splashes upward, O gold-heaper,
    And your purple shows your path!
But the child's sob in the silence curses deeper
    Than the strong man in his wrath.'

Hiram Powers' Greek Slave

They say Ideal beauty cannot enter
The house of anguish. On the threshold stands
An alien Image with enshackled hands,
Called the Greek Slave! as if the artist meant her
(That passionless perfection which he lent her,
Shadowed not darkened where the sill expands)
To, so, confront man's crimes in different lands
With man's ideal sense. Pierce to the centre,
Art's fiery finger! – and break up ere long
The serfdom of this world! appeal, fair stone,
From God's pure heights of beauty against man's wrong!
Catch up in thy divine face, not alone
East griefs but west, – and strike and shame the strong,
By thunders of white silence, overthrown.

A Note on Elizabeth Barrett Browning

Elizabeth Barrett Browning (1806–61), English Poet, born at Coxhoe Hall, Durham. Her early years were spent in Herefordshire, but later, after a financial setback of her father, the family lived in London. An accident at the age of 16 which injured her spine, the threat of consumption, and her father's sternness caused her to lead a sheltered and restricted life; in London she seldom left her room. A brief stay at Torquay with her brother Edward ended tragically with his death by drowning, 1840. In this cramping atmosphere her chief interests were literary. Her first published work, *The Battle of Marathon*, 1820, was much influenced by Pope's translation of Homer, although in later life she spoke disparagingly of her work in this and *An Essay on Mind, with other Poems*, 1826. Her translation of Aeschylus's *Prometheus Bound* was published in 1833 and *The Seraphim* in 1838; she also contributed to the *Athenaeum* and other periodicals. *Poems*, in two volumes, appeared in 1844.

Her reputation, by now established, led to a meeting with her future husband, Robert Browning, also a rising poet. The story of their love, vividly reflected in their own letters, has been retold in many novels and plays, the best known being Rudolph Besier's *The Barretts of Wimpole Street*, 1930. Browning's determination and optimism carried her off from her anxious family and possessive father to Italy, where her health dramatically improved. Their son was born in Florence. In 1850, four years after their marriage, a new and greatly enlarged edition of her *Poems* of 1844 appeared, containing the famous 'Sonnets from the Portuguese'. The name does not imply a translation but reflects a nickname, 'the little Portuguese', given to Elizabeth by her husband, to whom they were addressed and who thought them the finest in any language since Shakespeare. They are probably her best work, and their beauty of sentiment and musical phrasing is undeniable.

Casa Guidi Windows, 1851, reflects her eager response to the qualities of Italian life, and her sympathy with the aims of Italian patriotism. *Aurora Leigh*, 1857, is an important sociological romance or verse novel, an interesting departure from the lyricism of nearly all her previous work. Her husband's influence is discernible in this and in *Poems before Congress*, 1860. She died at Florence in 1861, and the next year a volume of *Last Poems* was issued. At her death she was far better known and more popular than her husband. Today the faults in her verse are more obvious than the good qualities with which they are linked – sentimentality together with her reforming zeal in 'The Cry of the Children'; a tendency to 'gush' together with romantic imagination in the 'Rhyme of the Duchess May'; volubility together with her easy command of words. She is often compared with Christina Rossetti, a more disciplined writer, whose success is therefore greater in the short lyrics at which both excelled. Her letters, both before and after marriage, are remarkable for their humour, tenderness, and descriptive skill.

Other titles in this series